Seasons Of Silence

My moments in poems

Ana Aguirre

BookLeaf Publishing

India | USA | UK

Made with ❤ on the BookLeaf Publishing Platform
www.bookleafpub.in
www.bookleafpub.com

Dedication

This book of poems is dedicated
to Paul, Sara, and Paulie.
You inspire me to write.

Preface

I have always been a writer (for fun). My writing focused mainly on my daughter. We have always had our ups and downs and my way to communicate with her was through writing.

The idea of writing poems came to me one day when I was feeling melancholy. Thus, my path to writing poems found its way to my paper. I would hear an interesting word(s) and voila I would develop a poem.

Poem writing has allowed me to put my heart into each one to express my raw emotions that I have experienced.

Acknowledgements

I want to give a big shout out to my husband Paul. He always encourages me in everything I pursue. Whether it is writing, painting, or learning a new language. He is always there cheering me on.

I also want to thank my children Sara and Paulie. You have inspired me to put my thoughts on paper.
Your love, patience, and forgiveness gives me hope for a brighter future.

Melancholy

Melancholy, hopeful for a
brighter side.
There's no book to follow and to
guide.
I must find my way.
But my strengths are buried deep
inside,
wanting to stay. Bursting
through the deep abyss to
keep moving forward as best as I
can.

Taking care of myself and finding
a place to land.
Healing my defeated soul and
heart,
keeping it quiet for a fresh start.

Forgiveness

How does forgiveness bring
relief? How do you forgive?
Carrying unresolved feelings will
trap you in a tunnel of loneliness
and despair.
Never able to move forward
towards a path of healing the
mind, heart, and soul.
The heavy chain of anger will
sink you to the dark abyss.
A place of uncertainty that can't
be missed.

You may not survive the
darkness of being trapped.
Letting go of the anger and
regrets to lift
to the surface and letting go of
the crap.
To live a life free of the past
history that has you stuck in
grief.
A renewed outlook to what can
be the most wonderful life like a
fresh fallin' leaf.
I forgive you, please forgive me.

Broken Lives

How do you repair Broken Lives?
Sorrow overwhelms me.
The wound opened with piercing
pain.
I'm a broken soul searching for
some peace,
to reconcile and not let our love
cease.
My life scattered into piles of
hurt and regret.
How am I going to repair our
Broken Lives?

I have no more to give.
My guilt overpowers me into a
sullenness.
Of darkness and loneliness.
Teetering on the precipice of
doom!
Will we ever heal from this
misery
and see our love bloom?
Moving forward to a place of
tranquility.
Doing away with all the hostility.

Intertwined Lives

We go through our day
loving our intertwined lives.
The many things we share and
say
warming our hearts with
words that will forever stay.
The friendly hugs and smiles,
that goes on for miles and miles.
Twenty plus years of memories
we have shared.
Sadness, joys, love, tears, and
fears.

Our intertwined lives will live on
in years.
Coming together here and there.
Always feels safe to be able to
share.
Like tree branches as they grow,
we reach for each other for
support when we are low.
Finding a safe haven, we help
each other through
the tough parts of life.
We laugh to celebrate the joys of
that is due.
Cheers to a friendship formed
long ago.

Our Intertwined Lives will
continue to grow.

Away You Go

I lost you many moons ago,

Like the waves that ebb and flow.

The waves coming to meet you

then leaving without

a word making me blue.

Away you go.

The heartache of waves

crash upon me row after row.

Disappointment wears on my

mind.

The waves of sadness anchor me

in a bind.

An emptiness surrounds the air.
Waiting for relief from the angry
stare.
A wish to start a new and
search for the times we once
knew.
Away you go.
The lovely memories linger in my
mind.
I want it to happen one more
time.
Happier days that we once had
Now fading forgotten to a lost
land.
One day we will rebuild and start
again.

A journey ready to begin.
Looking forward to a future filled
with love and laughter.
Desperately trying to avoid
disaster.
The waves will return and take
us to sunny places.
The wonderful memories that
will shine upon our faces.

Fog

My head is in a fog and it won't
lift away.
Birds flutter and tell me to stay.
Where am I going with this deep
seated feeling?
Trapped in myself waiting for the
healing.
The fog that surrounds me calls
out my name.
Shouting that I am not to blame.
Let go of the fog
to make your way back.

To a place that is quiet where
you once sat.

Hope

The twinkling lights are fading as
my mind
is on the brink of collapse.
I hold out hope for healing signs.
The sadness that has me in
straps.
I want to get rid of all this
madness that keeps me trapped.
Needing a vehicle to get on the
road to recovery.
Hoping to tell my healing story.
In the distance I can see the roads

calling to me to look forward.

As my mind starts to unfold.

Which road should I take?

That will help me find relief.

That will not cause me to break.

That will take away my grief.

Where will my mind find hope?

To reach my final destination.

To find my celebration.

The Wind Among the Trees

The wind among the trees rise
above me
telling me it's time to go.
Searching for a place to be loved.
A place to be understood.
Now my journey begins alone
and afraid.
But ready to meet it head on as I
should.
My tears carry me to different
places.

Searching, always searching for a
place to be loved.
The wind among the trees
reminds me that my time
will come and carry me to safety.
Be patient, be brave.
The wind among the trees
reminds me
to continue on my journey for it
will lead me to you,
my forever love.

Shadows

Shadows all around me,
casting me against a dark wall.
I gather my strength to not
crumble and fall.
The shadows follow me where I
go,
Not letting me be free and telling
me no.
They tell me don't leave me, stay
here.
But I must be free from you and
go elsewhere.

To discover myself from the
shadows that follow.
I need to leave before I am
swallowed.
The shadow slowly disappears
from my side.
Releasing me to be my own
guide.

Friendship

Friendships grow and bloom.
Friendships know when to look
up to the moon.
Friendships open up to the sun.
And you know they are the one.
You feel it in your heart.
This friendship will never part.
Friendships will be tethered to
my hem.
Each one gives me a piece of
them.

Lifting me up with words of
kindness.
The heartfelt talks that are
timeless.
Friendships old and new like
stars in the night sky.
Always bright and never saying
good-bye.
The growing vines of love
connect us to each other.
Our friendship opens up space
for one another.

Life Between Summers

My life between summers roll
and roll.
But when it appears the hot
season takes a toll.
The walk of freedom between
Fall and Spring.
Causes me to jump, cheer, and
sing.
Each summer brings a new time
to explore.
Willing to chase it more and
more.

The heat, the sunshine, and
summer fun.
Take it all in before it is done.
Until I see you again, my life
between summers.
I will keep watch for the little
hummers.
I will wait patiently for your
peaking rays.
Tell me what you have to say.

22 Years Old

22 years old, that's what you are
now.
Finding what you want in your
life
may take some time to figure out.
You accomplished many things,
so be proud of your hard work.
Show the world what you can
bring.
Along the way you will get what
you want.

Be patient, your dreams and
hopes
will surface to the top.
You will manage the chaos of life.
So be the best grown up you can
be.
The moment is yours to explore,
to be curious
about the sights you will see.

Son

You are following your own path,
building and growing your life.
Appreciating your world to smile
and laugh.
Son, continue on your way and
strive
to make your dreams come alive.
Pursue your incredible journey
for you to grow and be sturdy.
May all your hopes be fulfilled.
For this fantastic life you will
build.

The hardships you endured have
been worth the wait.
Now it's time to move forward
and make it great.

Wanting

Forgiveness wrapped in sorrow.
Hearts drowning in logs that are
so hollow.
Not knowing what to say and do.
Wanting you to love me
unconditionally so I can
stop feeling blue.
I made mistakes to atone.
Now I have to live with the
consequences all alone.
No rest, no relief insight. To
make it right.

Wanting a love that will never
be.
Needing to move along to a place
of sanity.
Never forgetting you, my love.
Now, you fly away like a dove.

Sara

You fluttered in gently 27 years
ago,
not knowing what this world
would hold.
You grabbed it and ran with it,
knowing you would succeed.
This world would not hold you
down
because you're a strong mustard
weed.
A seed that is hardy and strong
that can grow anywhere.

That's you my girl,
thriving and growing over there.
Keep fluttering and enjoy the
view
And don't ever stop being YOU!

Sara 2025

28 and flying high
The season of time has come to
say good-bye.
27 was fine,
but now it's time for your
moments to shine.
Ready for something great, so
take hold of the key,
something fabulous will come,
just wait and see.
Take delight in all the things
around you.

So all your dreams can come
true.
Let the sunshine be a guide to a
place.
Where drops of rays fall upon
your face.
It's wonderful to celebrate
another year
On the day that you arrived here.
Happy birthday!

Mistakes

Fixing mistakes that were made,
wanting my mistakes to fade.
Constantly failing to rise
and to make it alright.
My mistakes have taken me to an
unknown place
Filled with mountains of waste.
Trying desperately to be wanted
My hope to find peace and not be
taunted.
Mistakes take a toll on my mind,
constantly having me in a bind.

Will my mistakes ever go away
or forever stay?
Only I can answer and let go
before it swallows me whole.

Happy Life Lessons

Take away what life has taught

you.

Make it last to bring you

happiness.

The lessons along the way will

lift you,

to a place of a happy, content life.

Reach for it and learn that

happy Life Lessons will shine

upon you and bring you peace.

Raindrops

A few raindrop coming my way,
making me wish for a happy day.
The drops that fall and splash on
my face,
Reminds me of a long ago place.
Where life was easy a life long
ago,
when I was beginning to grow.
My life has had many changes,
where I was happy and sad.
At times making me afraid and
mad.

I have learned to accept my fate,
and proceed to a place with my
faith.
To rest my face and let those
raindrops keep me in my safe
space.

Journey

My journey had many detours.

Painful detours that encouraged

me to move along to the next

step in my life.

Happy, content detours that

really weren't good.

My false feeling made it seem

like it should.

I moved along to the next detour.

Trying to capture the direction of

self-love.

Searching for it to be enough.

I came upon you, someone who
gave me what I was looking for.
The detours that led me to where
I am now,
Gave me hope and made my
heart soar.

Finding Myself

The veil of self imposed defeat.
Trying to untie the knots that
kept me on my knees.
Realizing I must find the path
through the storm,
to live and stop being
emotionally torn.
I cleared my path to find Grace
for myself.
To detach the strings from the
guilt ridden well.

Finding relief for my mind and
heart.
Letting go of the thoughts that
are dark.
The ones that kept me down.
Breaking free from my regrets
that pound.
Learning to be content with what
I am.
Not able to change my life that
was and
move forward to a shelter that
will understand.
Realizing the past is gone,
looking to the future for a new
dawn.

I will no longer weep for the time
that is long gone.
It's time to take a stand
and fear no more the emotions at
hand.
Regret, guilt, and blame,
That puts me to shame.
My journey has been
excruciatingly hard to walk.
Learning along the way to
encourage myself with self-talk.
Remembering that only I can
make my way
To be grateful for the moments
that are here to stay.